Country Baking

Contents

Yeast Breads 4

Quick Breads 12

Rolls and Muffins 17

Pies and Custards 22

Cakes 28

Brownies 36

Bars 40

Drop Cookies 49

Shaped Cookies 56

Index 64

Created and manufactured by arrangement with Ideals Publishing Corp.
Copyright ©MCMLXXXV by Ideals Publishing Corp.
All rights reserved.
Manufactured in the United States of America.

Yeast Breads

White Bread
Makes 1 loaf

5½ to 6 cups all-purpose flour, divided
2 packages dry yeast
1 cup milk
1 cup water
2 tablespoons sugar
2 tablespoons oil
2 teaspoons salt
Oil

In a bowl, stir together 2 cups flour and yeast; set aside. In a saucepan, heat milk, water, sugar, 2 tablespoons oil, and salt to lukewarm (110° F.). Add liquid ingredients to flour-yeast mixture; beat until smooth. Stir in additional remaining flour to make a soft dough. Turn onto lightly floured board and knead until smooth, about 5 to 10 minutes. Cover dough and let rest 20 minutes. Punch down and form into a loaf. Place in a greased 9-inch loaf pan; brush with oil. Let rise until double in bulk, about 30 to 45 minutes. Bake in preheated 400° F. oven 35 to 40 minutes. Remove from pan immediately; brush with oil and cool on wire rack.

Oatmeal Bread
Makes 2 loaves

1 cup uncooked oatmeal
1 cup milk, scalded
½ cup boiling water
⅓ cup shortening
½ cup firmly packed brown sugar
2 teaspoons salt
2 packages dry yeast
½ cup warm water
5 cups sifted flour

In a large bowl, mix oatmeal, milk, and boiling water. Add shortening, sugar, and salt. Let stand until lukewarm. In a small bowl, sprinkle yeast on ½ cup warm water; stir until dissolved. Stir into oatmeal mixture; add half the flour and mix until smooth. Gradually add remaining flour until dough is moderately stiff. Turn out on lightly floured board and knead 7 minutes. Place dough in greased bowl, cover, and let rise 1½ hours. Punch down; knead and shape into loaves. Let rise until double in bulk. Bake at 400° F. for 10 minutes. Reduce heat to 350° F., and bake 40 minutes longer.

Raisin Braid
Makes 1 braid

3½ to 4 cups flour
1 package active dry yeast
¼ cup sugar
¼ teaspoon salt
1 cup whipping cream, lukewarm
2 eggs
1 egg white
1 teaspoon vanilla
1½ cups raisins
1 egg yolk
2 tablespoons milk

Sift flour into a large bowl. Sprinkle yeast onto flour; mix together. Blend in sugar, salt, cream, eggs, egg white, and vanilla. If dough becomes sticky, add flour, but dough must remain moderately soft. Place on a lightly floured board and knead until smooth. Place dough in a greased bowl; turn once to grease lightly. Cover and let rise 1½ hours or until doubled in bulk. Punch down dough. Turn out onto a lightly floured board and knead in raisins. Shape ⅔ of the dough into 3 rolls, each about 12 inches long. Braid the rolls together; place on a greased 10 x 15-inch cookie sheet. Beat egg yolk and milk together in a small bowl. Press a hollow along along the length of the braid with a rolling pin. Brush the hollow with the egg yolk mixture. From the remaining dough, form 3 rolls, each about 10 inches long; braid them together. Place this braid atop the hollow of the larger braid; brush with egg yolk mixture. Cover and let rise 45 minutes or until doubled in bulk. Bake in a preheated 375° F. oven 35 minutes or until golden brown and bottom sounds hollow when tapped. Remove from pan and cool on wire rack.

Mini-Loaves
Makes 4 mini-loaves

4 to 5 cups all-purpose flour, divided
2 packages dry yeast
¾ cup milk
1 cup water
2 tablespoons shortening
2 tablespoons sugar
2 teaspoons salt
1 egg
Melted butter, optional

Into a large mixing bowl, measure 2 cups flour; add yeast and mix. In a small saucepan, mix milk, water, shortening, sugar, and salt; heat until warm (120° to 130° F.). Pour into the flour-yeast mixture. Add egg and mix well. Gradually stir in enough of remaining flour to form a soft dough. Knead 5 to 10 minutes, until mixture is smooth. Cover dough and let rest 20 minutes. Divide dough into 4 equal parts. Shape into small loaves. Place in four 3 x 5 x 2-inch pans. Let rise until double in bulk, about 45 minutes. Bake 25 to 35 minutes in a preheated 400° F. oven. Remove from pans, and cool on racks. Brush with butter for soft crust, if desired.

Yeast Breads

Braided Fruit Bread
Makes 1 braid

3½ to 4 cups flour
1 package active dry yeast
⅓ cup sugar
¼ teaspoon salt
¾ cup sour cream at room temperature
½ cup milk, lukewarm
⅓ cup margarine, melted and cooled to lukewarm
1 teaspoon vanilla
4 slices canned pineapple, diced
1 cup raisins
½ cup flaked almonds

Into a large bowl, sift flour. Sprinkle with yeast and mix well. Blend in sugar, salt, sour cream, milk, margarine, and vanilla. Add flour if the dough is sticky, but dough must remain moderately soft. Place dough on lightly floured board and knead until smooth. Place dough in a greased bowl; turn once to grease lightly. Cover bowl and let dough rise 1½ hours or until doubled in bulk. Punch down dough. Divide into 3 equal portions. Knead pineapple into one portion, adding more flour only if needed. Knead raisins into a second portion, and almonds into the remaining portion. Shape each third into a 14-inch long roll. Braid the rolls together and place on greased 10 x 15-inch cookie sheet. Cover and let rise 45 minutes or until doubled in bulk. Brush the braid with water and bake in a preheated 375° F. oven for 35 minutes or until golden brown and bottom sounds hollow when tapped. Brush bread with water, remove from pan, and cool on wire rack.

Sesame Twist
Makes 2 loaves

5½ to 6 cups flour, divided
2 packages (¼ ounce each) active dry yeast
1 cup milk
1 cup water
2 tablespoons sugar
2 tablespoons vegetable oil
2 teaspoons salt
1 egg white beaten with 1 tablespoon water
Sesame seed

In a large bowl, stir together 2 cups flour and yeast. In a saucepan, combine milk, water, sugar, 2 tablespoons oil, and salt; heat over low heat until very warm (120 to 130° F.). Stir liquids into flour mixture. Beat on high speed of an electric mixer 3 minutes or until smooth. Stir in enough remaining flour to make a soft dough. Turn dough out onto a lightly floured surface. Knead until smooth and elastic, 8 to 10 minutes. Cover and let rise 20 minutes. Divide dough in 4 parts. Roll each part into a 15-inch rope. Wrap 2 ropes around each other in a spiral; tuck ends under. Repeat. Place in two greased 9 x 5-inch loaf pans. Brush tops with egg white mixture. Sprinkle with sesame seed. Cover and let rise in a warm draft-free place until doubled in bulk, 30 to 45 minutes. Preheat oven to 400° F. Bake 35 to 40 minutes or until loaves sound hollow when lightly tapped. Turn out of pans onto a wire rack to cool.

Yeast Breads

Cheese Bread
Makes 1 loaf

1 package active dry yeast
1 teaspoon sugar
1 cup lukewarm water
3 to 3½ cups wheat flour
1 teaspoon salt
⅛ teaspoon ground black pepper
3 tablespoons vegetable oil
¾ cup Emmenthaler cheese, cut into small cubes
⅓ cup Emmenthaler cheese, cut into wedges
1 egg yolk
1 tablespoon water

Sprinkle yeast and sugar in ½ cup of the lukewarm water; set aside for 5 minutes. Into a large bowl, sift flour, add salt and pepper. Pour in yeast mixture, remaining water, and oil. Mix well. If the dough is sticky, add a little flour, but dough must remain moderately soft. Place dough on a lightly floured board and knead until smooth. Place dough in a greased bowl; turn once to grease lightly. Cover and let rise 1½ hours or until doubled in bulk. Punch down dough. Place on pastry board and knead in the cubes of cheese until dough is smooth. Shape into a circle and place in an 8-inch greased soufflé dish. Insert cheese wedges into the dough. Cover and let rise 45 minutes or until doubled in bulk. In a small bowl, mix egg yolk and water. Brush top of bread with egg glaze. Bake in a preheated 400° F. oven 50 minutes or until bottom sounds hollow when tapped. Remove bread from dish; cool on wire rack.

Hearth Bread
Makes 2 large loaves

6 to 6½ cups all-purpose flour
2 packages dry yeast
2 cups water
2 tablespoons sugar
2 teaspoons salt
1 egg white, beaten
2 tablespoons water
Cornmeal

Stir together 2 cups flour and the yeast. In a saucepan, heat water, sugar, and salt until warm, 120° to 130° F. Add liquid ingredients to flour-yeast mixture and beat until smooth. Gradually add remaining flour to make a moderately stiff dough. Turn onto lightly floured surface; knead until smooth and elastic, 12 to 15 minutes. Cover dough and let rise 40 minutes. Punch down. Form into 2 loaves. Place on greased baking sheet, seam side down. With sharp knife, make diagonal cuts across top of loaves. Combine egg and water; brush on loaves. Sprinkle lightly with cornmeal. Let rise until double in bulk, about 20 to 30 minutes. Bake in preheated 375° F. oven 45 to 50 minutes. Brush tops with hot water after 20 minutes of baking; brush with water every 10 minutes until done.

Dilly Bread
Makes 1 loaf

2½ to 3 cups flour, divided
2 tablespoons sugar
2 to 3 teaspoons instant minced onion
2 teaspoons dill seed
1¼ teaspoons salt
¼ teaspoon baking soda
1 package (¼ ounce) active dry yeast
1 carton (8 ounces) cream-style cottage cheese
¼ cup lukewarm water (110° F.)
1 tablespoon butter *or* margarine
1 egg
Butter, softened

In a large mixing bowl, combine 1 cup flour, sugar, onion, dill seed, salt, baking soda, and yeast; set aside. In a saucepan, heat cottage cheese, water, and butter until very warm (120 to 130° F.). Add warm liquid and egg to flour mixture; blend on low speed of electric mixer until moistened, then beat 3 minutes at medium speed. Stir in remaining 1½ to 2 cups flour by hand to form a stiff batter. Place in a greased bowl; lightly oil top. Cover and let rise in warm, draft-free place until doubled in bulk, 45 to 65 minutes. Punch down. Turn dough into a well-greased 1½- or 2-quart casserole. Cover and let rise until doubled in bulk, 30 to 45 minutes. Preheat oven to 350° F. Bake 35 to 40 minutes or until golden. Turn out of casserole onto a wire rack to cool. Brush bread with butter while still warm.

Good Egg Bread
Makes 3 loaves

1½ cups scalded milk
½ cup butter
2 teaspoons salt
½ cup sugar
2 packages yeast
½ cup lukewarm water
2 beaten eggs
8 cups flour

Pour scalded milk over butter, salt, and sugar. Cool. Dissolve yeast in lukewarm water and let stand until it bubbles, about 5 minutes. Add yeast and beaten eggs to cooled milk. Gradually add flour, beating thoroughly. Use only enough flour to make a soft dough. Turn out on a lightly floured board and knead until smooth and elastic. Place in a greased bowl, cover, and let rise 1½ hours or until doubled in bulk. Punch down dough and shape into 3 loaves. Place in greased 8-inch loaf pans. Cover and let rise until dough is doubled in bulk. Bake in a preheated 425° F. oven for 10 minutes, then bake at 350° F. for 40 minutes more or until bread sounds hollow when tapped on the bottom.

Herb Bread
Makes 1 loaf

½ to ⅔ cup soft butter
2 teaspoons finely chopped onion
1 teaspoon chopped fresh parsley
1 teaspoon basil
1 teaspoon lemon juice
1 loaf of bread sliced ¾ through

Mix the first 5 ingredients and spread on the bread slices. Heat on a cookie sheet at 250° F. for 25 minutes. Separate slices before serving.

Almond Bread
Makes 1 loaf

3½ to 4 cups flour
1 package active dry yeast
⅓ cup sugar
¼ teaspoon salt
1 cup whipping cream, lukewarm
⅓ cup butter *or* margarine, melted and cooled to lukewarm
1 egg
1 teaspoon vanilla
1 cup raisins
1 cup almonds

Into a large bowl, sift flour; add yeast and mix. Blend in sugar, salt, cream, butter, egg, and vanilla. If dough becomes sticky, add flour, but dough must remain moderately soft. Place on a lightly floured board and knead until smooth. Place in a greased bowl; turn once to grease lightly. Cover and let rise 1½ hours or until doubled in bulk. Punch down dough. Turn out onto lightly floured board and knead until smooth. Knead in raisins and almonds. Shape dough into a loaf; place in a greased 9 x 5 x 3-inch loaf pan. Cover and let rise 45 minutes or until doubled in bulk. Brush loaf with water and bake in a preheated 375° F. oven for 35 minutes or until golden brown and bottom sounds hollow when tapped. Brush with water immediately after baking. Remove from pan and cool on wire rack.

Wheat Germ Bread
Makes 1 loaf

2¾ cups all-purpose flour, divided
2 packages dry yeast
½ cup wheat germ
1½ teaspoons salt
1 cup warm water
¼ cup molasses
2 tablespoons shortening
1 egg

In a large bowl, mix 1½ cups flour, yeast, wheat germ, and salt. Add water, molasses, shortening, and egg; mix again. Gradually stir in remaining flour to make a stiff dough. Cover; let rise until double in bulk, about 1 hour. Punch down dough. Place in greased 9-inch loaf pan or 2-quart casserole. Cover and let rise about 45 minutes. Bake in preheated 375° F. oven 35 to 50 minutes or until deep golden brown. Remove from pan and cool before slicing.

Quick Breads

Blueberry Coffee Cake
Makes 1 coffee cake

 1 **egg, lightly beaten**
10 **tablespoons sugar, divided**
1¼ **cups flour**
 2 **teaspoons baking powder**
 ¾ **teaspoon salt**
 ½ **cup milk**
 3 **tablespoons butter** or **margarine, melted**
 1 **cup fresh blueberries**
 1 **tablespoon butter** or **margarine, melted**

In a mixing bowl, blend egg and 8 tablespoons sugar. In a separate bowl, sift together flour, baking powder, and salt. Alternately add flour and milk to egg mixture; beat well after each addition. Stir in 3 tablespoons melted butter. Fold in blueberries. Turn batter into a greased 8-inch square baking pan. Sprinkle with remaining 2 tablespoons sugar. Cover and refrigerate overnight. Preheat oven to 350° F. Bake 35 minutes or until top springs back when lightly touched. Brush top with remaining butter. Cool in pan on a wire rack.

Quick Orange Coffee Cake
Makes 1 coffee cake

 ⅔ **cup sugar**
 1 **tablespoon grated orange peel**
 2 **packages (10 ounces each) refrigerated buttermilk biscuits**
 3 **tablespoons butter** or **margarine, melted**
 ½ **cup powdered sugar**
 1 **tablespoon orange juice**

In a small bowl, mix together sugar and orange peel; set aside. Separate biscuits. Dip each into melted butter, then into sugar mixture to coat well. In a greased 9-inch round baking pan, arrange dough to overlap slightly. Sprinkle any remaining sugar mixture on top. Bake in a preheated 375° F. oven 35 minutes or until golden brown. Cool on a wire rack 10 minutes. Turn out onto a serving plate. In a small bowl, combine powdered sugar and orange juice; blend well. Drizzle over coffee cake.

Cinnamon Coffee Round

Makes 1 coffee cake

¾ **cup sugar**
6 **tablespoons vegetable shortening**
1 **egg**
2 **cups flour**
2 **teaspoons baking powder**
1 **teaspoon salt**
1 **cup milk**
Streusel Topping

In a mixing bowl, cream sugar and shortening until light and fluffy. Beat in egg. In a separate bowl, sift together flour, baking powder, and salt. Alternately add flour mixture and milk to creamed mixture; blend well after each addition. Stir in half of the Streusel Topping. Spread batter into a greased 8-inch round baking pan. Smooth top of dough. Sprinkle with remaining Streusel Topping. Bake in a preheated 350° F. oven 30 to 35 minutes or until a wooden pick inserted in the center comes out clean. Serve warm.

Streusel Topping

½ **cup sugar**
2 **tablespoons flour**
1 **tablespoon ground cinnamon**
2 **tablespoons butter** *or* **margarine, melted**
¾ **cup chopped nuts**
⅓ **cup raisins, optional**

In a small bowl, combine all ingredients; stir until blended.

Dark Pineapple Date Bread

Makes 1 loaf

2 **cups all-purpose flour**
¼ **cup firmly packed light brown sugar**
1 **tablespoon baking powder**
1 **teaspoon salt**
1 **8-ounce can crushed pineapple (do not drain)**
1¼ **cups (8 ounces) chopped, pitted dates**
1 **cup chopped pecans**
2 **eggs**
⅔ **cup milk**
¼ **cup vegetable oil**

In a large bowl, stir together flour, sugar, baking powder, and salt; set aside. In a small saucepan combine pineapple with liquid and dates; cook over low heat, stirring until liquid is absorbed and mixture is dark and thick. Stir in nuts. Cool 10 minutes. In another bowl, combine eggs, milk, and oil; add date mixture. Stir until smooth. Add liquid ingredients to flour mixture, stirring only until flour is moistened. Pour batter into a greased 9 x 5-inch loaf pan. Bake in a preheated 350° F. oven 60 to 70 minutes. Cover pan with foil the last 15 minutes of baking to prevent excessive browning. Cool 10 minutes in pan. Invert onto wire rack to cool completely.

Quick Breads

Lemon Bread
Makes 1 loaf

3 tablespoons margarine
1 cup sugar
½ teaspoon salt
2 eggs
1½ cups sifted flour
1 teaspoon baking powder
½ cup milk
1 tablespoon grated lemon peel
   Juice of 1 lemon
½ cup sugar

In a small bowl, cream margarine, sugar, and salt. Add egg, and set aside. In another bowl, stir together flour and baking powder. Add flour and milk alternately to creamed mixture, mixing well after each addition. Add lemon peel; pour batter into a greased 9 x 5-inch loaf pan. Bake in a preheated 350° F. oven for 55 minutes or until a wooden pick inserted in the center comes out clean. In a saucepan, heat lemon juice and sugar until sugar dissolves. Remove loaf from pan while still hot, and drizzle lemon mixture over the top.

Applesauce Nut Bread
Makes 1 loaf

2 cups flour
¾ cup sugar
1 tablespoon baking powder
1 teaspoon salt
½ teaspoon baking soda
½ teaspoon ground cinnamon
1 egg, lightly beaten
1 cup applesauce
2 tablespoons vegetable
   shortening, melted
1 cup chopped nuts

In a bowl, sift together flour, sugar, baking powder, salt, baking soda, and cinnamon; set aside. In another bowl, combine egg, applesauce, and melted shortening; blend well. Gradually add flour mixture; blend well. Stir in nuts. Turn batter into a greased 9 x 5-inch loaf pan. Bake in a preheated 350° F. oven 1 hour or until a wooden pick inserted in the center comes out clean. Cool in pan 10 minutes. Invert onto a wire rack to cool completely.

Apricot Bread
Makes 1 loaf

2 cups flour
1 cup sugar
2½ teaspoons baking powder
¾ teaspoon salt
¾ cup crunchy nut-like cereal
⅔ cup chopped dried apricots
1 egg
1¼ cups milk
2 tablespoons vegetable
   shortening, melted

In a large bowl, mix flour, sugar, baking powder, and salt. Stir in cereal and apricots. In a small bowl, beat together egg and milk. Stir in melted shortening. Add liquids to flour mixture; stir until evenly moist. Turn batter into a greased 9 x 5-inch loaf pan. Bake in a preheated 350° F. oven 1 hour or until a wooden pick inserted in the center comes out clean. Cool in pan 10 minutes. Invert onto a wire rack to cool completely.

Quick Breads

Pumpkin Bread
Makes 2 loaves

3 cups sugar
1 cup vegetable oil
4 eggs, lightly beaten
2 cups canned pumpkin
3½ cups flour
2 teaspoons baking soda
1 teaspoon baking powder
1 teaspoon salt
1 teaspoon nutmeg
1 teaspoon ground allspice
1 teaspoon ground cinnamon
½ teaspoon ground cloves
⅔ cup water

In a large mixing bowl, combine sugar, oil, eggs, and pumpkin; blend well. In a separate bowl, combine flour, baking soda, baking powder, salt, nutmeg, allspice, cinnamon, and cloves. Alternately add flour mixture and water to pumpkin mixture, beginning and ending with flour; blend well after each addition. Pour batter into two greased 9 x 5-inch loaf pans. Bake in a preheated 350° F. oven 1½ hours or until a wooden pick inserted in the center comes out clean. Cool in pans 10 minutes. Invert onto a wire rack to cool completely.

Carrot Bread
Makes 1 loaf

¾ cup vegetable oil
1 cup sugar
2 eggs
1½ cups flour
¼ teaspoon salt
1 teaspoon baking soda
1 teaspoon ground cinnamon
1 cup grated carrots
1 cup chopped dates
1 cup chopped nuts

In a large bowl, combine oil, sugar, and eggs; blend well. In a separate bowl, mix together flour, salt, baking soda, and cinnamon. Alternately add flour mixture and carrots to sugar mixture; blend well after each addition. Stir in dates and nuts. Pour batter into a greased 9 x 5 inch loaf pan. Bake in a preheated 350° F. oven 1 hour or until a wooden pick inserted in the center comes out clean. Cool in pan 10 minutes. Invert onto a wire rack to cool completely.

Date Bread
Makes 1 loaf

1 package (2 cups) dates, chopped
1½ cups boiling water
2 cups sugar
1 tablespoon butter
1 tablespoon vanilla
1 egg
3 cups flour
2 teaspoons baking soda
1 teaspoon salt
1 cup chopped pecans

Place dates in boiling water and set aside. In a large bowl, cream sugar, butter, and vanilla; add egg and mix well. In another bowl, stir together flour, baking soda, and salt. Add flour to creamed mixture; stir until just moistened. Drain dates well. Add dates and pecans to dough. Pour into a greased 9 x 5-inch loaf pan. Bake in a preheated 400° F. oven for 15 minutes; then turn down heat to 300° F. and bake 1½ hours or until a wooden pick inserted in the center comes out clean. Let bread cool in pan 10 minutes. Invert on wire rack and let cool completely.

Rolls and Muffins

Savory Bread Rolls
Makes 1 dozen

1 package active dry yeast
1 teaspoon sugar
1 cup lukewarm water
3 to 3½ cups wheat flour
1 teaspoon salt
⅛ teaspoon ground pepper
3 tablespoons vegetable oil
2 tablespoons chopped parsley
2 tablespoons chopped chives
1 teaspoon chopped dill
1 egg yolk
1 teaspoon water

Sprinkle yeast and sugar into water, stir to dissolve, and set aside. Sift flour into a large bowl; add salt and pepper. Pour in yeast mixture; stir in oil and mix well. If dough becomes sticky, add flour, but dough must remain moderately soft. Place on a lightly floured board and knead until smooth. Place dough in a greased bowl; turn once to grease lightly. Cover and let rise 45 minutes. Punch down dough. Knead in herbs until smooth. Shape dough into 12 equal rolls. Place on a greased 10 x 15-inch cookie sheet. Cover and let rise 45 minutes or until doubled in bulk. Cut two ¼-inch deep slashes in the top of each roll, forming a cross. Combine egg yolk and water. Brush tops of rolls with mixture. Bake in a preheated 350° F. oven for 25 minutes or until rolls are golden brown and sound hollow when tapped.

Poppy Seed Muffins
Makes about 1½ dozen

¾ cup sugar
¼ cup butter or margarine, softened
½ teaspoon grated orange peel
2 eggs
2 cup flour
2½ teaspoons baking powder
½ teaspoon salt
¼ teaspoon ground nutmeg
1 cup milk
½ cup golden raisins
½ cup chopped pecans
¼ cup poppy seed

In a large mixing bowl, cream sugar, butter, and orange peel until light and fluffy. Add eggs, one at a time, beating well after each addition. In a separate bowl, combine flour, baking powder, salt, and nutmeg. Alternately add flour mixture and milk to creamed mixture; blend well after each addition. Stir in raisins, nuts, and poppy seed. Fill greased muffin cups ¾ full with batter. Bake at 400° F. 20 minutes or until golden.

Banana Muffins

Makes 1 dozen

2	cups sifted all-purpose flour
⅓	cup sugar
2	teaspoons baking powder
1½	teaspoons cinnamon
1	teaspoon salt
1	cup milk
1	cup mashed ripe bananas
1	egg, beaten
¼	cup melted shortening
1	tablespoon sugar
¼	teaspoon cinnamon

Into a bowl, sift flour, sugar, baking powder, cinnamon, and salt; set aside. In another bowl, combine milk, bananas, egg, and shortening; add all at once to flour mixture, stirring only until dry ingredients are moistened. The batter will be lumpy. Fill greased muffin tins ⅔ full. Mix together remaining 1 tablespoon sugar and ¼ teaspoon cinnamon; sprinkle on top of each muffin. Bake in a preheated 400° F. oven for 25 minutes.

Pecan Rolls

Makes 1 dozen

½	cup milk
4	tablespoons butter *or* margarine
⅓	cup granulated sugar
½	teaspoon salt
1	egg, lightly beaten
¼	cup lukewarm water (110° F.)
1	package (¼ ounce) active dry yeast
1	teaspoon granulated sugar
2½	to 3 cups flour, divided
3	tablespoons butter, melted
1	teaspoon ground cinnamon
6	tablespoons granulated sugar
½	cup packed brown sugar
1	cup chopped pecans

In a saucepan, scald milk. Add 4 tablespoons butter, ⅓ cup sugar, and salt; stir until butter melts. Cool to room temperature. Stir in egg; set aside. In a bowl, sprinkle yeast and 1 teaspoon sugar over water; let stand 5 minutes. In a large mixing bowl, combine milk and yeast mixtures. Stir in 1 cup of the flour to make a soft batter. Gradually stir in remaining flour to make a stiff dough. Turn dough out onto a lightly floured surface. Knead until smooth and elastic, 8 to 10 minutes. Place dough in a greased bowl; turn once to grease top. Cover and let rise until doubled in bulk, about 1½ hours. Roll out dough into a 16 x 8-inch rectangle. Brush top with 3 tablespoons melted butter. In a small bowl, combine cinnamon and 6 tablespoons granulated sugar. Sprinkle cinnamon mixture over dough. Roll up tightly from the long side. Cut into 12 pieces. Generously grease a 12-cup muffin tin. Sprinkle ½ cup brown sugar in muffin cups. Divide pecans among muffin cups. Place a piece of dough, cut side down, in each muffin cup. Cover and let rise 30 minutes. Preheat oven to 375° F. Bake 15 minutes or until golden. Turn out rolls onto a wire rack to cool.

Rolls and Muffins

Cinnamon Rounds

Makes about 1 dozen

- **1 package active dry yeast**
- **¼ cup lukewarm water**
- **3 cups flour**
- **¼ teaspoon salt**
- **2 tablespoons sugar**
- **1 cup butter or margarine at room temperature**
- **½ cup milk, lukewarm**
- **1 egg, slightly beaten**
- **3 tablespoons vegetable oil**
- **½ cup sugar**
- **½ cup firmly packed brown sugar**
- **2 tablespoons ground cinnamon**

Sprinkle yeast over water; set aside. In a large bowl, mix flour, salt, and 2 tablespoons sugar. Cut in butter with a pastry blender or 2 knives; set aside. In another bowl, blend milk, egg, and oil; stir in yeast mixture. pour milk mixture over flour; stir only until all ingredients are moistened. Cover and chill for 1 hour. Turn out dough onto a lightly floured board; knead 4 or 5 times. Roll out dough to form an 11" x 8" rectangle. In a small bowl, mix remaining sugars and cinnamon. Sprinkle ½ of the mixture over dough. Roll up the dough tightly, beginning on a long side. Pinch edges to seal. Wrap in plastic wrap; chill for 1 hour. Cut dough into ½-inch slices. Sprinkle both sides of each slice with remaining sugar mixture. Flatten each slice into a 5-inch circle. Sprinkle with more sugar if dough is sticky. Place dough circles on a 10 x 15-inch non-stick cookie sheet. Bake in a preheated 400° F. oven for 10 to 12 minutes or until lightly browned. Place on wire rack to cool.

Breakfast Rolls

Makes 1 dozen

- **¾ cup milk, lukewarm**
- **1 package active dry yeast**
- **2 teaspoons sugar**
- **3½ to 4 cups flour**
- **¾ cup sugar**
- **¼ teaspoon salt**
- **¼ cup butter or margarine, melted and cooled to lukewarm**
- **1 egg, beaten**
- **1 teaspoon vanilla**
- **2 tablespoons butter or margarine**

Pour lukewarm milk into a small bowl. Stir in yeast and 2 teaspoons sugar; set aside. Into a large bowl, sift flour. Make a hollow in the center and add ¾ cup sugar, salt, melted butter, egg, vanilla, and yeast mixture; mix well. If the dough becomes sticky, add flour, but dough must remain moderately soft. Place dough on a lightly floured board and knead until smooth. Place in a greased bowl; turn once to grease lightly. Cover and let rise 1½ hours or until doubled in bulk. Punch down dough. Turn out onto a lightly floured board and knead until smooth. Form dough into 12 equal balls. Melt remaining 2 tablespoons butter in a pie plate. Roll the dough balls in the butter; cover and let rise 25 minutes or until doubled in bulk. Bake in a preheated 400° F. oven for 25 to 30 minutes or until rolls are golden brown and sound hollow when bottom is tapped. Remove and cool on wire rack.

Cranberry Orange Muffins
Makes about 1 dozen

2 cups flour
½ teaspoon salt
1½ teaspoons baking powder
½ teaspoon baking soda
¼ cup sugar
⅔ cup boiling water
2 tablespoons butter *or* margarine
1 egg, lightly beaten
1 cup cranberry relish
1 tablespoon grated orange peel

Into a large bowl, sift together flour, salt, baking powder, baking soda, and sugar; set aside. Stir butter into boiling water. Cool to room temperature. Stir egg into water. Gradually add liquids to dry ingredients; blend well. Stir in cranberry relish and orange peel. Fill greased muffin cups ⅔ full with batter. Bake at 425° F. 40 to 45 minutes or until golden.

Oatmeal Muffins
Makes 1 dozen

1½ cups flour
¼ cup sugar
4 teaspoons baking powder
½ teaspoon salt
¾ cups oatmeal
1 egg beaten
1 cup milk
3 tablespoons melted shortening
½ cup raisins

In a large bowl, mix and sift flour, sugar, baking powder, and salt. Add remaining ingredients; beat well. Fill greased muffin tins about ⅔ full. Bake in a preheated 400° F. oven 15 to 20 minutes.

Bran Muffins
Makes 6 dozen

2 cups boiling water
2 cups bran
2½ cups sugar
1 cup vegetable shortening
4 eggs, lightly beaten
1 quart buttermilk
5 cups flour
5 teaspoons baking soda
½ teaspoon salt
4 cups coarsely crushed bran cereal

In a bowl, pour boiling water over bran; let stand 5 minutes. In a mixing bowl, cream sugar and shortening until light and fluffy. Add eggs, buttermilk, and bran mixture; blend well. In a separate bowl, combine flour, baking soda, salt, and bran cereal. Gradually add to liquid mixture, blending well after each addition. Fill greased muffin cups about ⅔ full with batter. Bake at 400° F. 15 to 20 minutes or until golden. Can be stored in refrigerator up to 5 weeks.

Pies and Custards

Piecrust*
Makes 2 piecrusts or 1 double crust pie

1 cup vegetable shortening **3 cups sifted flour** **1½ teaspoon salt** **½ cup ice water**	In a mixing bowl, cut shortening into flour and salt using a pastry blender or two knives until consistency of small peas. Blend in water, 1 tablespoon at a time, tossing with a fork. Gather dough into a ball.

*This recipe can be used for all pies in this chapter calling for piecrust.

Lemon Lattice Pie
Makes 1 pie

2 cups sugar **¼ cup plus 2 tablespoons flour** **6 eggs, beaten** **½ cup butter** **1 cup lemon juice** **2 teaspoons grated lemon peel** **1 9-inch unbaked pastry shell** **Lattice**	Mix sugar and flour in top of double boiler; beat in eggs, butter, lemon juice and lemon peel. Cook, stirring constantly, 12 to 15 minutes or until mixture thickens. Cool. Pour into pie shell; set aside. Prepare Lattice; weave into lattice design on top of custard-filled pie shell. Preheat oven to 350°. Bake 30 to 35 minutes until golden brown. Cool on rack.

Lattice

1 cup flour **½ cup light brown sugar, packed** **1 teaspoon baking powder** **¼ teaspoon ground nutmeg** **¼ cup butter *or* margarine** **1 egg, lightly beaten** **1 tablespoon milk**	Mix flour, sugar, baking powder, and nutmeg in bowl; cut in butter until mixture resembles small peas. Stir in egg and milk. Knead slightly; form into ball. Chill 30 minutes. Roll dough into 11-inch circle on lightly floured surface; cut into strips.

Plum Pie, page 24
Pink Ribbon Apple Pie, page 25

Pies and Custards

Pecan Pie
Makes 1 pie

3 **eggs**
½ **cup sugar**
1 **cup dark corn syrup**
⅛ **teaspoon salt**
1 **teaspoon vanilla**
¼ **cup butter** *or* **margarine, melted**
1 **cup whole pecans**
1 **unbaked 9-inch pastry shell**

Beat eggs in a bowl; add sugar and syrup. Beat in salt, vanilla, and butter; set aside. Spread pecans evenly in bottom of pie shell; add filling. Bake in a preheated 350° F. oven 50 to 60 minutes. Nuts will rise to top of pie to form crust. Cool on rack.

Plum Pie
Makes 1 pie

Pastry for 9-inch double piecrust
4 **cups sliced plums**
1 **tablespoon lemon juice**
½ **teaspoon almond extract**
¼ **cup butter** *or* **margarine**
¼ **cup flour**
1½ **cups sugar**

Roll half of pastry and line a 9-inch pie pan; set aside. Gently toss plums with lemon juice and almond extract; place in pie shell. Dot with butter. In a small bowl, combine flour and sugar; sprinkle over fruit. Roll remaining pastry to fit over pie; seal edges. Cut slits in top to vent steam. Bake in a preheated 450° F. oven 35 to 45 minutes until brown and bubbly. Cool on rack.

Sweet Potato Pie
Makes 1 pie

3 **cups cooked sweet potatoes, pureed**
1 **cup firmly packed light brown sugar**
½ **teaspoon cinnamon**
¼ **teaspoon each allspice, nutmeg, and salt**
3 **eggs, beaten**
½ **pint half-and-half**
4 **tablespoons melted butter**
1 **unbaked 9-inch pie shell**

In a bowl, mix all ingredients except pie shell. Mound into unbaked pie shell; smooth surface with a spatula. Bake in a preheated 450° F. oven 10 minutes; reduce heat to 250° F. and continue baking for 20 minutes or until wooden pick inserted in center comes out clean. Serve hot or cold.

Pink Ribbon Apple Pie

Makes 1 pie

8 to 9 tart apples, sliced
¼ cup lemon juice
Piecrust
1½ to 2 cups sugar
3 tablespoons flour
1 teaspoon salt
1 teaspoon ground cinnamon
½ teaspoon ground nutmeg
Butter

Slice apples; place in a bowl of ice water with lemon juice. Prepare piecrust. Divide dough. Roll out one half on a floured pastry cloth 1 inch larger than a 9-inch pie plate. Fit dough into pie plate. Drain apples on paper towels. Place a layer of apples in prepared pie plate. In a small bowl, combine sugar, flour, salt, cinnamon, and nutmeg; blend well. Sprinkle some of the sugar mixture over apple layer; dot with butter. Repeat layers until all apples are used, ending with sugar mixture and butter. Roll out remaining dough. Place on top of apples. Press top and bottom crusts together; trim and flute edge. Cut slits in the top to vent steam. Bake on middle rack in oven at 400° F. 10 minutes. Reduce heat to 350° F. and bake 40 minutes or until bubbly and golden.

Rhubarb Custard Dessert

Makes one 18 x 12-inch pie

Crust (recipe follows)
6 eggs, separated
2¾ cups sugar, divided
1 cup half-and-half *or* milk*
¼ cup flour
6 cups chopped rhubarb
½ cup chopped nuts, optional
½ cup shredded coconut, optional

Prepare crust; pat into an 18 x 12-inch baking pan. Bake at 350° F. 10 minutes. Remove from oven; let stand until cool. In a large mixing bowl, combine egg yolks, 2 cups sugar, half-and-half, and flour; blend well. Stir in rhubarb. Pour custard mixture evenly over cooled crust. Bake at 350° F. 40 minutes or until set. In a small mixing bowl, beat egg whites with an electric mixer until foamy. Gradually add remaining ¾ cup sugar, beating until stiff peaks form. Spread meringue on top of rhubarb custard, being certain to seal edges. Sprinkle with nuts and coconut, if desired. Bake 10 to 12 minutes or until lightly browned.

*If using milk, add 1 whole egg to custard.

Crust

1 cup vegetable shortening
2 cups flour
2 tablespoons sugar

In a mixing bowl, cut shortening into flour and sugar using a pastry blender or two knives until consistency of coarse crumbs.

Pies and Custards

Sour Cream Pumpkin Pie

Makes 1 pie

1 cup firmly packed light brown sugar
1 tablespoon flour
½ teaspoon salt
1 teaspoon ground ginger
½ teaspoon ground nutmeg
½ teaspoon ground cloves
½ teaspoon ground cinnamon
1 cup canned pumpkin
2 eggs, well beaten
1 cup evaporated milk
½ cup dairy sour cream
½ cup chopped walnuts
1 unbaked 9-inch pastry shell
   Whipped cream, optional

In a bowl mix brown sugar, flour, salt, and spices. Add pumpkin, eggs, milk, sour cream, and walnuts; mix well. Pour into crust. Bake in a preheated 400° F. oven 40 to 50 minutes or until knife inserted in center comes out clean. Cool on rack. Edge crust with whipped cream, if desired.

Fresh Cherry Pie

Makes 1 pie

   Pastry for 9-inch double piecrust
1⅓ cups sugar
⅓ cup flour
⅛ teaspoon salt
4 cups pitted tart cherries
3 drops almond extract, optional
2 tablespoons butter or margarine

Divide piecrust dough in half. Roll out half and fit into a 9-inch pie plate; set aside. In a small bowl, combine sugar, flour, and salt; set aside. In a separate bowl, combine cherries and almond extract. Sprinkle with flour mixture; toss lightly to mix. Turn cherry mixture into prepared crust. Dot with butter. Roll out remaining dough. Cut into ½-inch strips. Weave strips into a lattice top. Trim, seal, and flute edge. Bake in a preheated 425° F. oven 40 minutes or until bubbly.

Deep Dish Strawberry-Rhubarb Pie

Makes 1 pie

3 cups ½-inch rhubarb pieces
2 cups sliced strawberries
1 tablespoon lemon juice
1½ cups sugar
3 tablespoons tapioca
½ teaspoon vanilla
2 tablespoons butter or margarine
   Pastry for 9-inch single piecrust
1 tablespoon sugar

Place fruits and lemon juice in an 8-inch square baking dish. Combine 1½ cups sugar and tapioca; toss gently with fruit. Sprinkle with vanilla and dot with butter. Roll pastry to 9-inch square and place over fruit. Crimp at edge of pan to seal; cut 3 slits to vent steam. Sprinkle with 1 tablespoon sugar. Bake in a preheated 400° F. oven 45 to 50 minutes until crust is golden brown. Cool on rack.

Cakes

Apple Streusel Cake
Makes one 9 x 13-inch cake

1	cup milk, lukewarm
1	package active dry yeast
2	teaspoons sugar
3½ to 4	cups flour
¼	cup sugar
¼	teaspoon salt
¼	cup butter *or* margarine, melted and cooled to lukewarm
1	teaspoon vanilla
3½	cups peeled, thinly sliced cooking apples
½	cup slivered almonds
½	cup golden raisins
1	teaspoon cinnamon
⅛	cup sugar

Into a small bowl, pour lukewarm milk. Add yeast and sugar, stirring until dissolved; set aside for 5 minutes. Into a large bowl, sift flour. Make a hollow in the center. Add ¼ cup sugar, salt, butter, vanilla, and the yeast mixture in the hollow. Mix well. If the dough is sticky, add flour, but the dough must remain moderately soft. Place dough on a lightly floured board and knead until smooth. Place dough in a greased bowl; turn once to grease lightly. Cover and let rise 45 minutes or until doubled in bulk. Punch down dough. Pat into greased 9 x 13-inch cake pan. Arrange apple slices on top of dough. Cover and let rise 45 minutes or until doubled in bulk. Sprinkle top with almonds, raisins, cinnamon, and ⅛ cup sugar. Bake in a preheated 375° F. oven 25 to 30 minutes or until golden brown. Remove from pan; cool on wire rack. To serve, cut into 2 x 3-inch strips.

Chocolate Dream Cake
Makes one 9 x 13-inch cake

1¾	cups sifted cake flour
1½	cups sugar
1	teaspoon baking soda
1	teaspoon salt
½	cup sifted cocoa
½	cup butter, softened
1	cup buttermilk, divided
2	eggs

In a large bowl, combine flour, sugar, baking soda, salt, and cocoa. Add butter and ⅔ cup buttermilk; mix well. Add eggs and remaining buttermilk; mix well. Pour into a greased 9 x 13-inch baking pan. Bake in a preheated 350° F. oven about 30 minutes. Cool 10 minutes. Remove from pan; cool on wire rack.

Almond Chiffon Cake
Makes one 10-inch tube cake

2	**cups sifted all-purpose flour**
1½	**cups sugar**
1	**tablespoon baking powder**
1	**teaspoon salt**
7	**eggs, separated**
½	**cup vegetable oil**
1	**teaspoon lemon extract**
1	**teaspoon almond extract**
¾	**cup ice water**
½	**teaspoon cream of tartar**
	Double Boiler Frosting
	Sliced almonds

In a bowl, sift first 4 ingredients together four times; set aside. In another bowl, combine egg yolks, vegetable oil, extracts, and ice water. Add dry ingredients; mix well and set aside. Beat egg whites and cream of tartar until stiff peaks form. Gradually fold egg whites into flour mixture. Pour into ungreased 10-inch tube pan. Bake in a preheated 325° F. oven for 55 minutes; increase temperature to 350° F. and bake 10 minutes longer. Invert to cool for 1½ to 2 hours. Ice with Double Boiler Frosting, and sprinkle sliced almonds on top.

Double Boiler Frosting

2	**egg whites**
1½	**cups sugar**
¼	**teaspoon cream of tartar**
⅓	**cup water**
1	**teaspoon vanilla**

Combine egg whites, sugar, cream of tartar, and water in top of double boiler. Beat on high for 1 minute with electric mixer. Place over boiling water and beat on high speed for seven minutes. Remove pan from boiling water. Add vanilla. Beat 2 minutes longer on high speed. Spread on cake.

Glazed Williamsburg Pound Cake
Makes one 10-inch tube cake

2	**cups butter, softened**
3	**cups sugar**
12	**egg yolks, well beaten**
12	**egg whites, beaten to stiff peaks**
4	**cups all-purpose flour, sifted**
	Cranberry Glaze
	Whole cranberries, optional

In a bowl, cream butter and sugar. Alternately add egg yolks, egg whites, and flour to butter mixture. Beat until light and smooth. Pour into greased and floured 10-inch tube pan. Bake in preheated 325° F. oven about 1½ hours or until golden brown. Cool in pan 30 minutes before removing. Drizzle cooled Cranberry Glaze over cake. Decorate with whole cranberries, if desired.

Cranberry Glaze

2	**cups water**
2	**cups sugar**
1	**pound (4 cups) cranberries**

In a saucepan, bring water and sugar to rapid boil. Simmer 10 minutes. Add cranberries. Cook until cranberries pop, about 5 minutes. Remove cranberries with slotted spoon to a small bowl (store in refrigerator for another use). Continue to cook syrup until thickened, about 20 minutes. Cool before using.

Old-Fashioned Pound Cake
Makes one 10-inch tube cake

2 **cups butter** *or* **margarine**
3½ **cups sugar**
10 **eggs**
4 **cups flour**
1 **teaspoon vanilla**
   Lemon Glaze

In a large mixing bowl, cream butter and sugar until light and fluffy. Add eggs, one at a time, beating well after each addition. Gradually add flour; blend well. Pour batter into a greased 10-inch tube pan. Bake in a preheated 300° F. oven 2 hours or until a wooden pick inserted near the center comes out clean. Cool in pan 10 minutes before turning out onto a wire rack to cool completely. Drizzle Lemon Glaze over the top.

Lemon Glaze

2 **tablespoons butter** *or*
   margarine
4 **teaspoons lemon juice**
1 **cup sifted powdered sugar**

In a small bowl, combine sugar, lemon juice, and butter; blend until smooth. Let glaze stand for 3 to 4 minutes to thicken.

Frosty Spice Cake
Makes one 8-inch cake

½ **cup shortening**
1 **cup sugar**
2 **eggs**
2¼ **cups sifted cake flour**
2 **teaspoons cinnamon**
1 **teaspoon baking powder**
1 **teaspoon cloves**
½ **teaspoon baking soda**
1 **teaspoon salt**
¼ **teaspoon nutmeg**
⅛ **teaspoon allspice**
1 **cup dairy sour cream**
   Frosty Icing
⅓ **cup chopped walnuts**

In a large bowl, cream shortening and sugar. Add eggs, one at a time, beating well after each; set aside. In another bowl, sift together dry ingredients; add to creamed mixture alternately with sour cream. Pour into two greased 8-inch cake pans. Bake in a preheated 375° F. oven 25 to 30 minutes. Cool; frost with Frosty Icing. Sprinkle with walnuts.

Frosty Icing

1 **cup packed light brown sugar**
2 **egg whites**
3 **tablespoons cold water**
½ **teaspoon vanilla**

In the top of a double boiler, mix sugar, egg whites, and water. Place over boiling water. Beat constantly with electric mixer until stiff peaks form, 4 to 5 minutes. Remove top pan from heat. Add vanilla; beat 1 minute longer. Spread on cake immediately.

Cakes

Plum Crazy Cake
Makes one 9-inch cake

3 cups pitted and quartered plums
1⅔ cups sugar, divided
2 tablespoons cornstarch
1 teaspoon orange peel
½ cup orange juice
½ cup water
¼ cup butter
1 egg
2 cups sifted all-purpose flour
1 tablespoon baking powder
¼ teaspoon salt
1 cup milk
Sweetened whipped cream

Arrange plums, skin side down, in a 9-inch square baking pan. In a 2-quart saucepan, mix 1 cup sugar and cornstarch; gradually add orange peel, juice, and water. Cook over medium heat, stirring until thickened. Cook 2 additional minutes. Pour over plums. In a bowl, cream butter and remaining sugar. Beat in egg; set aside. In another bowl, sift together flour, baking powder, and salt; add to creamed mixture alternately with milk. Carefully spoon mixture over top of plums; spread evenly to cover orange mixture. Bake in preheated 350° F. oven 45 minutes. Cool in pan on wire rack 5 minutes. Invert onto serving plate so that plums are on the top. Serve with whipped cream.

Carrot Cake
Makes one 9 x 13-inch cake

2 cups flour
2 teaspoons baking soda
2 teaspoons ground cinnamon
1½ teaspoons salt
2 cups sugar
1½ cups vegetable oil
4 eggs
1 tablespoon vanilla
3 cups grated carrots
1 cup chopped pitted dates
1 cup flaked coconut
1 cup raisins, optional
1 cup chopped nuts, optional
Cream Cheese Frosting

In a medium bowl, sift together flour, baking soda, cinnamon, and salt; set aside. In a large mixing bowl, combine sugar and oil; blend well. Beat in eggs, one at a time, until well blended. Stir in vanilla. Gradually add dry ingredients; beat until well blended. Stir in carrots, dates, coconut, raisins, and nuts, if desired. Pour batter into a greased 9 x 13-inch baking pan. Bake at 350° F. for 30 to 40 minutes or until center springs back when lightly touched. Cool on a wire rack. Frost with Cream Cheese Frosting.

Cream Cheese Frosting

2 packages (3 ounces each) cream cheese, softened
6 tablespoons butter or margarine, softened
1 tablespoon milk
1 teaspoon vanilla
4 cups sifted powdered sugar

In a mixing bowl, combine cream cheese and butter; cream with electric mixer until light and fluffy. Beat in milk and vanilla. Gradually beat in powdered sugar until of spreading consistency.

Carrot Cake with Pineapple

Makes one 10-inch tube cake

2	**cups sugar**
1⅓	**cups vegetable oil**
3	**eggs, beaten**
3	**cups flour**
2	**teaspoons baking soda**
2	**teaspoons cinnamon**
1	**teaspoon salt**
2	**cups grated carrots**
1	**cup chopped walnuts** *or* **pecans**
1	**cup drained crushed pineapple**
2	**teaspoons vanilla**
	Lemon Glaze

In a small bowl, blend sugar, oil, and eggs; set aside. In a large bowl, sift together flour, soda, cinnamon, and salt. Make a hollow in the dry mixture and pour in the sugar mixture; mix well. Add the carrots, nuts, pineapple and vanilla. Pour the batter into an ungreased 10-inch tube pan, and bake in a preheated 350° F. oven for an hour and 15 minutes. Cool cake in pan 15 minutes; loosen sides and remove from pan. Ice with Lemon Glaze.

Lemon Glaze

1	**cup powdered sugar, sifted**
2	**tablespoons lemon juice**
3	**tablespoons butter, melted**

In a small bowl, combine sugar, lemon juice, and butter; blend until smooth. Let glaze stand for 3 to 4 minutes to thicken.

Yeast Pound Cake

Makes 1 bundt cake

¾	**cup whipping cream, lukewarm**
1	**package active dry yeast**
2	**teaspoons sugar**
3½	**cups flour**
¾	**cup sugar**
¾	**cup ground almonds**
	Peel of ½ lemon, grated
¾	**cup butter** *or* **margarine, melted and cooled to lukewarm**
3	**eggs**
1	**teaspoon vanilla**
1½	**cups raisins**
3	**tablespoons slivered almonds**
	Powdered sugar

Into a small bowl, pour whipping cream. Stir in yeast and 2 teaspoons sugar; set aside for 5 minutes. Into a large bowl, sift flour. Make a hollow in the center and add ¾ cup sugar, ground almonds, lemon peel, butter, eggs, vanilla, and yeast mixture; mix well. If the dough becomes sticky, add flour, but dough must remain moderately soft. Place dough on a lightly floured board; knead in raisins. Sprinkle almonds in the bottom of a greased bundt pan. Spread dough evenly in pan. Let rise 2½ hours or until doubled in bulk. Bake in a preheated 350° F. oven 40 to 45 minutes or until a wooden pick inserted in center comes out clean. Turn out cake onto wire rack to cool, dust generously with powdered sugar.

Cakes

Potato Cake

Makes one 9 x 13-inch cake

1 cup butter *or* margarine, softened
2 cups sugar
4 eggs, separated
1 cup unseasoned mashed potatoes
1 cup chopped nuts
1 teaspoon ground cinnamon
1 teaspoon ground cloves
1 teaspoon ground nutmeg
2½ cups flour
2 teaspoons baking powder
½ cup milk

In a large mixing bowl, cream butter and sugar with an electric mixer until light and fluffy. Add egg yolks, potatoes, nuts, and spices; blend well. In a separate bowl, combine flour and baking powder. Alternately add flour mixture and milk to creamed mixture; blend well. In a small bowl, beat egg whites with electric mixer until stiff peaks form. Gently fold egg whites into batter. Pour batter into a greased and floured 9 x 13-inch baking pan. Bake in a preheated 350° F. oven 45 minutes or until a toothpick inserted in the center comes out clean.

Honey Cake

Makes one 8-inch cake

½ cup sugar
½ cup butter *or* margarine
2 eggs
½ cup honey
¾ cup milk
1 teaspoon almond flavoring
2 cups flour
2½ teaspoons baking powder
½ teaspoon mace
½ teaspoon salt
Honey Nut Topping
Whipped cream, optional

In a large bowl, cream sugar and butter. Add eggs, one at a time, beating after each addition. Beat in honey; set aside. In a small bowl, combine milk and almond flavoring; set aside. In another bowl, sift together flour, baking powder, mace, and salt; add to creamed mixture alternately with milk, beating well after each addition. Pour batter into two greased and floured 8-inch round cake pans. Bake in a preheated 350° F. oven 35 minutes. Spread layers with Honey Nut Topping and bake about 5 minutes longer. Cool; remove from pans. Stack layers and frost with whipped cream, if desired.

Honey Nut Topping

⅓ cup honey
½ cup chopped nuts
¼ cup brown sugar
½ teaspoon cinnamon
¼ cup softened butter

Mix together all ingredients and spread on hot layers.

Brownies

Blonde Brownies

Makes 1½ dozen

½ cup butter, softened
1 cup sugar
1 egg yolk
1 whole egg
1 teaspoon vanilla
2 cups all-purpose flour
1 teaspoon baking powder
½ teaspoon salt
1 cup packed brown sugar
1 cup chopped walnuts
1 egg white

In a large mixing bowl, cream butter and sugar until smooth. Add egg yolk, whole egg, and vanilla; blend well. Sift together flour, baking powder, and salt. Gradually add to creamed mixture, beating until well blended. Pour batter into a greased 9-inch square baking pan. Stir together brown sugar, nuts, and egg white. Spread over the batter. Bake at 325° F. for 1 hour or until brownie begins to pull away from sides of the pan. Cool in pan before cutting into squares.

Light Nut Brownies

Makes 3 dozen

¼ butter *or* margarine, softened
1 cup all-purpose flour
¼ teaspoon salt
2 eggs
¾ cup packed light brown sugar
1 cup chopped walnuts, divided
1 teaspoon vanilla
2 tablespoons all-purpose flour
Chocolate Frosting

In a large mixing bowl, cream butter. Gradually add 1 cup flour and salt; blend well. Spread the batter in a greased and floured 9-inch square baking pan. Bake at 350° F. for 15 minutes; cool. In a small bowl, beat eggs and sugar until light. Stir in ¾ cup nuts, vanilla, and 2 tablespoons flour. Spoon over cooled crust. Return to oven. Bake at 350° F. for 15 minutes. Cool in pan. Spread with Chocolate Frosting. Sprinkle with remaining ¼ cup nuts. Cut into squares.

Chocolate Frosting

1 cup semisweet chocolate chips
¼ cup light corn syrup
1 tablespoon water

In the top of a double boiler, melt chocolate chips over hot but not boiling water. Blend in corn syrup and water.

Toffee Crunch Brownies
Makes 2 dozen

4 squares (1 ounce each) unsweetened baking chocolate
½ cup butter
4 eggs
1 cup sugar
2 teaspoons vanilla
¾ cup all-purpose flour
¼ teaspoon salt
6 ounces toffee candy bars, chopped

In the top of a double boiler, melt chocolate and butter over warm water. Remove from heat. In a large mixing bowl, beat eggs and sugar until light and fluffy; blend into chocolate mixture. Blend in vanilla, flour, and salt. Stir in toffee candy. Spoon mixture into a greased 9-inch square baking pan. Bake at 325° F. for 45 minutes. Cool in pan before cutting into squares.

Two-Toned Brownies
Makes about 1½ dozen

¼ cup butter *or* margarine, softened
¼ cup sugar
¼ cup light corn syrup
1 egg
1 cup all-purpose flour
½ teaspoon baking powder
¼ teaspoon salt
2 squares (1 ounce each) semisweet chocolate, melted
1 package (3 ounces) cream cheese, softened

In a large mixing bowl, cream butter and sugar until smooth. Blend in corn syrup and egg. Combine flour, baking powder, and salt. Add dry ingredients to creamed mixture; blend well. To ½ cup of the batter blend in melted chocolate. To remaining batter, add cream cheese; beat until smooth. Spread cream cheese batter in a greased 9-inch square baking pan. Carefully spread chocolate batter on top. With a knife, swirl chocolate batter through cream cheese batter. Bake at 350° F. for 40 to 45 minutes or until brownie begins to pull away from sides of the pan. Cool in pan before cutting into squares.

Best Fudge Nut Brownies
Makes 1 dozen

4 squares (1 ounce each) unsweetened baking chocolate
1 cup butter *or* margarine
2 cups sugar
3 eggs, lightly beaten
2 teaspoons vanilla
½ teaspoon salt
1 cup chopped nuts
1 cup sifted flour

Preheat oven to 350° F. In a small saucepan, melt chocolate and butter over low heat, stirring constantly. Add sugar and eggs; blend well. Stir in vanilla, salt, and nuts. Gradually add flour; blend well. Pour into a greased and floured 9-inch square baking pan. Bake 40 to 45 minutes or until brownie begins to pull away from edge of pan. Cool in pan on a wire rack. Cut into squares.

Moist Chocolate Brownies
Makes 1½ dozen

1 **box (8 ounces) semisweet chocolate**
7 **tablespoons butter**
2 **eggs**
¾ **cup sugar**
1 **teaspoon vanilla**
¼ **cup all-purpose flour**
1 **cup coarsely chopped walnuts**

In the top of a double boiler, melt chocolate and butter over warm water. Remove from heat. In a large mixing bowl, beat eggs and sugar until light and fluffy. Blend in chocolate mixture and vanilla. Stir in flour and nuts. Pour batter into a greased 8-inch square baking pan. Bake at 375° F. for 30 minutes or until brownie begins to pull away from sides of the pan. Cool in pan before cutting into squares.

Marshmallow Pecan Brownies
Makes 3 dozen

2 **squares (1 ounce each) unsweetened baking chocolate**
½ **cup butter** *or* **margarine**
2 **eggs**
1 **cup sugar**
1 **teaspoon vanilla**
1¼ **cups sifted all-purpose flour**
½ **teaspoon baking powder**
½ **teaspoon salt**
1 **cup chopped pecans**
2 **cups miniature marshmallows**
Mocha Chocolate Frosting

In a small saucepan, melt chocolate and butter over low heat, stirring constantly; set aside to cool. In a large mixing bowl, beat eggs lightly. Blend in sugar, vanilla, and melted chocolate mixture. Stir together flour, baking powder, and salt; gradually blend into chocolate mixture. Stir in pecans. Spread batter in a greased 11 x 7-inch baking pan. Bake at 325° F. for 25 minutes or until brownie begins to pull away from sides of the pan. Sprinkle marshmallows evenly over top. Return to oven for 3 to 4 minutes or until marshmallows are soft. Cool before spreading with Mocha Chocolate Frosting. Cut into 2 x 1-inch bars.

Mocha Chocolate Frosting

1 **square (1 ounce) unsweetened chocolate**
2 **tablespoons butter**
1 **teaspoon instant coffee granules**
½ **teaspoon vanilla**
⅛ **teaspoon salt**
2 **cups powdered sugar**
2 **to 3 tablespoons hot water**

In a small saucepan, melt chocolate and butter over low heat, stirring constantly. Blend in coffee, vanilla, and salt. Gradually beat in powdered sugar, adding water, if necessary, to bring to spreading consistency.

Bars

Pumpkin Bars
Makes 3 dozen

4 eggs
1 cup vegetable oil
2 cups sugar
1 can (15 ounces) pumpkin
2 cups flour
2 teaspoons baking powder
1 teaspoon baking soda
½ teaspoon salt
2 teaspoons ground cinnamon
½ teaspoon ground ginger
½ teaspoon ground cloves
½ teaspoon ground nutmeg
½ cup chopped nuts
   Cream Cheese Frosting

In a large bowl, combine eggs, oil, sugar, and pumpkin; blend well. In a separate bowl, sift together flour, baking powder, baking soda, salt, and spices. Gradually beat flour mixture into pumpkin mixture. Stir in nuts. Pour batter into greased and floured 18 x 12-inch pan. Bake at 350° F. 25 to 30 minutes or until center springs back when touched lightly. Cool on a wire rack before frosting with Creamed Cheese Frosting.

Cream Cheese Frosting

6 ounces cream cheese, softened
6 tablespoons butter *or* margarine, softened
1 tablespoon milk
1 teaspoon vanilla
4 cups sifted powdered sugar

In a mixing bowl, combine cream cheese and butter; cream until light and fluffy. Beat in milk and vanilla. Gradually beat in powdered sugar until of spreading consistency.

English Toffee Bars
Makes about 6 dozen

1 cup butter, softened
1 cup sugar
1 egg yolk
1¾ cups all-purpose flour
1 teaspoon cinnamon
1 egg white, lightly beaten
1 cup chopped pecans
3 tablespoons milk
1 teaspoon instant coffee granules
2 squares (1 ounce each) semisweet chocolate

In a large bowl, cream butter and sugar until smooth. Add egg yolk; blend well. Sift together flour and cinnamon. Gradually work dry ingredients into creamed mixture until crumbly. Press crumb mixture evenly into a buttered 15 x 10-inch baking pan. Brush top with egg white. Sprinkle with pecans; press lightly into dough. Bake at 275° F. for 1 hour. While the crust is baking, heat milk, coffee granules, and chocolate in a saucepan over low heat, stirring until chocolate melts. Cut into 1½-inch bars. Drizzle with melted chocolate mixture. Cool in pan on a wire rack.

Filbert Chocolate Cream Bars
Makes 3 dozen

1 cup chopped filberts *or* almonds
½ cup butter
¼ cup sugar
2 tablespoons unsweetened cocoa
2 teaspoons vanilla
¼ teaspoon salt
1 egg, beaten
1¾ cups vanilla wafer crumbs (about 45 wafers)
½ cup flaked coconut
Mint Frosting
4 squares (1 ounce each) semisweet baking chocolate

Spread nuts in a shallow baking pan. Toast in oven for 5 to 10 minutes, stirring occasionally. In a medium saucepan, combine butter, sugar, cocoa, vanilla, salt, and egg. Cook over low heat, stirring constantly until mixture thickens and becomes glossy. Combine cookie crumbs, nuts, and coconut. Add cocoa mixture; blend well. Press firmly into a 9-inch square baking pan. Spread Mint Frosting on top. Chill until frosting is firm. In the top of a double boiler, melt chocolate over hot but not boiling water. Spread chocolate over frosting. Let stand until chocolate is partially set. Cut into bars. Refrigerate until ready to serve.

Mint Frosting

¼ cup butter, softened
1 egg
½ teaspoon peppermint extract
2 cups sifted powdered sugar

In a small mixing bowl, cream butter and egg until smooth. Blend in peppermint extract. Gradually add powdered sugar, beating until smooth and creamy.

Peanut Brittle Bars
Makes 3 dozen

 1 **cup all-purpose flour**
 ¼ **teaspoon baking soda**
 ½ **teaspoon cinnamon**
 ½ **cup butter, softened**
 ½ **cup packed light brown sugar**
 1 **teaspoon vanilla**
 1 **egg, beaten**
 1 **cup finely chopped salted peanuts, divided**

Sift together flour, baking soda, and cinnamon; set aside. In a large mixing bowl, cream butter and brown sugar until smooth. Blend in vanilla and 2 tablespoons of the egg; reserve remaining egg. Gradually add dry ingredients, blending well. Stir in ½ cup peanuts. Spread batter in a greased 14 x 10-inch baking pan. Brush with reserved egg. Sprinkle with remaining ½ cup peanuts. Bake at 325° F. for 20 minutes. Cool in pan 5 minutes before cutting into bars.

Orange Bars
Makes 3 dozen

 ½ **cup butter, softened**
1½ **cups all-purpose flour**
 ¼ **cup sugar**
 3 **tablespoons grated orange peel**
 1 **egg**
 1 **package (6 ounces) semisweet chocolate chips**

In a large mixing bowl, cut butter into flour until crumbly. Blend in sugar, orange peel, and egg. Roll out dough on a lightly floured surface to a ¼-inch thickness. Cut into 2 x 1-inch bars. Place bars about 1 inch apart on a lightly greased baking sheet. Bake at 400° F. for 8 to 10 minutes or until lightly browned. Remove from baking sheet to a wire rack to cool. Melt chocolate in the top of a double boiler over hot but not boiling water. Dip each bar halfway into the melted chocolate. Place on a sheet of waxed paper until the chocolate sets, about 10 minutes.

Pear and Graham Cracker Bars
Makes about 2½ dozen

 2 **ripe Bartlett pears**
    Whole graham crackers
 1 **cup packed light brown sugar**
 ½ **cup butter** *or* **margarine**
 ¼ **cup milk**
 1 **cup flaked coconut**
 1 **cup graham cracker crumbs**
 1 **package (6 ounces) butterscotch chips**

Core and dice pears to measure 1½ cups. Line a 13 x 9-inch baking pan with whole graham crackers. In a medium saucepan, combine diced pears, brown sugar, butter, milk, coconut, and graham cracker crumbs; bring to a boil. Boil until thick, stirring constantly. Spread pear mixture over crackers. Top with layer of whole crackers. In the top of a double boiler, melt butterscotch chips. Spread melted chips over crackers. Cut between crackers into bars. Store in the refrigerator.

Bars

Date Chocolate Chip Bars

Makes 1 dozen

1 package (8 ounces) pitted
  dates, chopped
½ cup sugar
1 cup water
⅔ cup butter *or* margarine
1 cup packed brown sugar
1½ cups quick-cooking oats
1 teaspoon baking soda
1 tablespoon hot water
1½ cups flour
½ cup chopped nuts
½ cup semisweet chocolate chips
  Sweetened whipped cream,
  optional

In a medium saucepan, combine dates, sugar, and water. Cook over medium heat until thick, stirring constantly. In a mixing bowl, combine butter and brown sugar. Cream with an electric mixer until light and fluffy. Add oats, baking soda, and hot water; blend well. Gradually add flour; blend well. Reserve 1 cup oat mixture for topping. Press remaining mixture into an ungreased 13 x 9-inch baking pan. Spread date mixture evenly over top. Sprinkle with nuts, chocolate chips, and reserved mixture; pat lightly. Bake at 350° F. 20 to 25 minutes or until golden. Serve warm or cool topped with whipped cream, if desired.

Chocolate Chip Butterscotch Bars

Makes 2 dozen

¾ cup all-purpose flour
½ teaspoon baking powder
½ teaspoon salt
½ cup butter *or* margarine
1 cup packed dark brown sugar
2 eggs
1 teaspoon vanilla
2½ cups semisweet chocolate
  chips, divided
½ cup chopped walnuts
  Butterscotch Frosting

Stir together flour, baking powder, and salt; set aside. In a medium saucepan, melt butter. Add brown sugar; stir over low heat until sugar melts. Transfer to a large mixing bowl. Add eggs, 1 at a time, beating well after each addition. Blend in vanilla. Add dry ingredients; blend well. Stir in 2 cups chocolate chips and nuts. Spread batter in a greased 8-inch square baking pan. Bake at 350° F. for 30 minutes. Cool in pan. Frost with Butterscotch Frosting. Sprinkle with remaining ½ cup chocolate chips. Cut into bars.

Butterscotch Frosting

¼ cup butter *or* margarine,
  softened
½ cup packed dark brown sugar
1 tablespoon half-and-half
¼ teaspoon vanilla

In a small mixing bowl, cream butter and sugar until smooth. Blend in cream and vanilla. If frosting is too soft to spread, chill 10 minutes before using.

Raspberry Bars
Makes 2 dozen

¾ cup margarine, softened
1 cup packed light brown sugar
1¾ cups all-purpose flour
½ teaspoon baking soda
½ teaspoon salt
1½ cups rolled oats
1 jar (18 ounces) raspberry jam

In a large mixing bowl, cream margarine and brown sugar until smooth. In another bowl, stir together flour, baking soda, and salt. Gradually add dry ingredients to creamed mixture; mix until crumbly. Stir in oats. Press half of the crumb mixture into a greased 13 x 9-inch baking pan. Spread with raspberry jam. Sprinkle remaining crumb mixture over the top; press lightly into jam. Bake at 400° F. for 20 minutes or until lightly browned. Cool 5 minutes before cutting into bars.

Spice Bars
Makes about 2 dozen

1 cup water
1 cup sugar
1 cup raisins
½ cup butter
  Salt, to taste
2 cups flour
1 teaspoon baking soda
1 teaspoon cinnamon
½ teaspoon nutmeg
½ teaspoon cloves
½ cup chopped dates
½ cup walnuts, chopped
  Powdered sugar

In a saucepan, mix first 5 ingredients and bring to a boil; let cool. In a bowl, mix flour, baking soda, and spices. Combine the cooled raisin mixture with the flour mixture. Add the dates and walnuts. Spread on a greased 13 x 9-inch cookie sheet and bake in a preheated 350° F. oven 25 minutes. Sprinkle with powdered sugar while warm.

Irish Mist Bars
Makes 1½ dozen

½ cup butter, softened
1½ cups packed light brown sugar, divided
1 cup all-purpose flour
1 tablespoon all-purpose flour
¼ teaspoon salt
2 eggs
1 tablespoon Irish Mist liqueur
1 cup chopped nuts

In a large mixing bowl, combine butter, ½ cup brown sugar, and 1 cup flour; blend until crumbly. Firmly press crumb mixture into a 9-inch square baking pan. Bake at 350° F. for 10 minutes; set aside to cool. In a large mixing bowl, combine remaining 1 cup brown sugar, 1 tablespoon flour, and salt; blend well. Add eggs, 1 at a time, beating well after each addition. Blend in liqueur; stir in nuts. Spread batter evenly over cooled crust. Bake at 350° F. for 20 minutes. Cool in pan before cutting into bars.

Bars

Jeweled Coconut Chews
Makes about 1½ dozen

⅓ cup butter *or* margarine, softened
⅓ cup powdered sugar
¾ cup all-purpose flour
1 cup seedless green grapes
½ cup packed brown sugar
¼ cup chopped walnuts
¼ cup flaked coconut
1 tablespoon flour
1 egg
¼ teaspoon baking powder
¼ teaspoon salt
¼ teaspoon almond extract
⅛ teaspoon nutmeg

In a small mixing bowl, cream butter and powdered sugar until smooth. Add ¾ cup flour; mix until crumbly. Press crumb mixture into an ungreased 8-inch square baking pan. Bake at 350° F. for 15 minutes or until light brown. In a large bowl, combine remaining ingredients; blend well. Spread over baked crust. Bake at 350° F. for 25 minutes or until golden brown. Cool in pan before cutting into bars.

Fruit Bars
Makes 2 dozen

½ cup butter, softened
1 cup sugar
2 eggs
1 teaspoon vanilla
¾ cup all-purpose flour
1 teaspoon baking powder
¼ teaspoon salt
1 cup chopped walnuts
½ cup red candied cherries, halved
1 cup sliced pitted dates
½ cup sliced soft dried apricots
½ cup sliced soft dried figs
Chocolate Glaze

In a large mixing bowl, cream butter and sugar until smooth. Add eggs, 1 at a time, beating well after each addition. Blend in vanilla. In another bowl, stir together flour, baking powder, and salt. Gradually add dry ingredients to creamed mixture; blend well. Stir in nuts and fruit. Spread batter in a greased 9-inch square baking pan. Bake at 350° F. for 45 minutes. Cool in pan before cutting into bars. Spread with Chocolate Glaze. Store in an airtight container.

Chocolate Glaze

⅓ cup sugar
3 tablespoons water
1 cup semisweet chocolate chips
3 tablespoons marshmallow creme
1 to 2 tablespoons hot water

In a small saucepan, combine sugar and 3 tablespoons water. Bring to a boil; remove from heat. Stir in chocolate chips until melted. Blend in marshmallow creme. Add hot water, 1 teaspoonful at a time, stirring until desired consistency is reached.

Bars

Double Chocolate Crumble Bars
Makes about 4 dozen

½ cup butter, softened
¾ cup sugar
2 eggs
1 teaspoon vanilla
¾ cup all-purpose flour
½ cup chopped pecans
2 tablespoons unsweetened cocoa
¼ teaspoon baking powder
¼ teaspoon salt
2 cups miniature marshmallows
1 package (6 ounces) semisweet chocolate chips
1 cup peanut butter
1½ cups crispy rice cereal

In a large mixing bowl, cream butter and sugar until smooth. Blend in eggs and vanilla. Stir together flour, pecans, cocoa, baking powder, and salt. Gradually add dry ingredients to the creamed mixture; blend well. Spread batter in a greased 13 x 9-inch baking pan. Bake at 350° F. for 15 to 20 minutes or until light brown. Sprinkle marshmallows evenly over top. Bake for 3 minutes. Cool in pan on a wire rack. In a small saucepan, melt chocolate chips and peanut butter over low heat, stirring constantly. Stir in cereal. Spread on top of cooled crust. Refrigerate until firm. Cut into bars. Store in the refrigerator.

Almond Squares
Makes 2½ dozen

3½ to 4 cups flour
1 package active dry yeast
⅔ cup sugar, divided
¼ teaspoon salt
1 cup milk, lukewarm
¾ cup butter or margarine, melted, cooled to lukewarm, and divided
2 teaspoons vanilla, divided
½ cup flaked almonds
Sugar

Sift flour into a large bowl; sprinkle yeast over flour and mix well. Blend in ⅓ cup sugar, salt, milk, ¼ cup butter, and 1 teaspoon vanilla. Add more flour if the dough becomes sticky, but dough should remain soft. Place dough on a lightly floured board and knead until smooth. Move dough to a greased bowl; turn once to grease lightly. Cover bowl and put in a warm place for 1½ hours or until dough doubles in bulk. Punch down, and turn out onto a lightly floured board; knead until smooth. Roll out dough to fit a greased 10 x 15-inch cookie sheet; place on cookie sheet. Brush remaining butter over dough. Combine remaining sugar and vanilla; sprinkle over dough. Sprinkle on almonds. Cover and let rise for 45 minutes or until doubled in bulk. Bake in a preheated 350° F. oven for 35 minutes or until golden brown. Sprinkle with sugar. Remove from sheet and cool on wire rack. Cut into squares.

Drop Cookies

Thumbprint Cookies
Makes about 3 dozen

1 cup granulated sugar
1 cup brown sugar
1¼ cups margarine
3 eggs
2 teaspoons vanilla
4 cups sifted flour
1 teaspoon salt
1 teaspoon baking soda
1 teaspoon baking powder
1 teaspoon cinnamon
1 cup chopped dates, optional
1 cup chopped nuts, optional
¼ cup warm water
　Orange marmalade *or*
　strawberry preserves

Cream sugars and margarine. Add eggs and vanilla and beat well; set aside. In a large bowl, sift together flour, salt, baking soda, baking powder, and cinnamon. Add dry ingredients to creamed mixture. Mix in dates and nuts, if desired. Add the warm water. Drop by tablespoons onto ungreased cookie sheet. Make a thumbprint in the center of each cookie, and fill indentations with marmalade or strawberry preserves. Bake in a preheated 375° F. oven for 12 minutes.

Drop Sugar Cookies
Makes about 5 dozen

⅔ cup vegetable shortening
1⅔ cups sugar
2 eggs
2 teaspoons vanilla
3½ cups sifted all-purpose flour
½ teaspoon baking soda
1 teaspoon salt
2 teaspoons baking powder
½ cup dairy sour cream

In a large mixing bowl, cream shortening and sugar until smooth. Add eggs and vanilla; blend well. In another bowl, stir together flour, baking soda, salt, and baking powder. Add dry ingredients alternately with sour cream to creamed mixture, beating well after each addition. Drop batter by teaspoonfuls 2 inches apart onto an ungreased baking sheet. Bake at 375° F. for 12 minutes or until just golden. Remove from baking sheet to a wire rack to cool.

Cranberry Charms

Makes about 6 dozen

2 cups fresh cranberries, coarsely chopped
1 cup granulated sugar, divided
1 cup vegetable shortening
1¼ cups packed light brown sugar
2 eggs
1¾ cups all-purpose flour
1 teaspoon salt
1 teaspoon baking powder
1 teaspoon baking soda
1 teaspoon cinnamon
1 teaspoon nutmeg
½ cup buttermilk *or* sour milk*
1 teaspoon vanilla
1 tablespoon grated orange peel
3 cups rolled oats
1 cup chopped nuts

In a small bowl, combine cranberries and ¾ cup granulated sugar; set aside for 30 minutes. In a large mixing bowl, cream remaining ¼ cup granulated sugar, shortening, brown sugar, and eggs until blended. Stir together flour, salt, baking powder, baking soda, and spices. Add dry ingredients alternately with buttermilk and vanilla to creamed mixture, beating well after each addition. Stir in orange peel, oats, nuts, and 1 cup of the cranberry-sugar mixture. Drop batter by tablespoonfuls 2 inches apart onto a greased baking sheet. Top cookies with remaining chopped cranberries. Bake at 400° F. for 10 minutes or until cookies are brown around the edges.

*To sour milk, mix 1½ teaspoons lemon juice into milk to equal ½ cup.

Golden Apple Cookies

Makes about 3½ dozen

1 cup vegetable shortening
¾ cup granulated sugar
¾ cup packed brown sugar
3 eggs
1 tablespoon grated orange peel
2 cups all-purpose flour
2 teaspoons baking powder
1 teaspoon cinnamon
½ teaspoon cloves
½ teaspoon nutmeg
½ teaspoon salt
3 or 4 Golden Delicious apples
2 cups rolled oats
½ cup raisins
½ cup chopped nuts

In a large mixing bowl, cream shortening and sugars until smooth. Blend in eggs and orange peel. Combine flour, baking powder, spices, and salt. Gradually add dry ingredients to creamed mixture; blend well. Pare, core, and chop apples to equal 3 cups. Stir in apples, oats, raisins, and nuts. Drop batter by rounded tablespoonfuls 2 inches apart onto a greased baking sheet. Bake at 350° F. for 15 to 17 minutes or until lightly browned. Remove from baking sheet to a wire rack to cool.

Drop Cookies

Applesauce Cookies
Makes 5 dozen

1¾ **cups all-purpose flour**
½ **teaspoon baking powder**
1 **teaspoon baking soda**
¼ **teaspoon salt**
1 **teaspoon cinnamon**
½ **teaspoon cloves**
½ **teaspoon nutmeg**
¾ **cup butter** *or* **margarine, softened**
1 **cup sugar**
1 **egg**
1 **cup thick sweetened applesauce**
½ **cup raisins**
1 **cup cornflakes, crushed**

Combine flour, baking powder, baking soda, salt, and spices; set aside. In a large mixing bowl, cream butter and sugar until smooth. Blend in egg. Add dry ingredients alternately with applesauce to creamed mixture, beating after each addition. Stir in raisins and cereal. Drop batter by teaspoonfuls about 2 inches apart onto a greased and floured baking sheet. Bake at 375° F. for 10 minutes or until golden. Remove from baking sheet to a wire rack to cool.

Anise Drops
Makes 4 dozen

1½ **cups all-purpose flour**
¼ **teaspoon baking powder**
2 **eggs**
1 **cup sugar**
¼ **teaspoon anise extract**

Combine flour and baking powder; set aside. In a large mixing bowl, beat eggs, sugar, and anise extract until light-colored. Stir in dry ingredients. Drop batter by teaspoonfuls about 2 inches apart onto a greased and floured baking sheet. Let stand at room temperature for 6 hours. Bake at 350° F. for 6 minutes. Remove from baking sheet to a wire rack to cool.

Currant Cakes
Makes 3 dozen

1 **cup butter, softened**
1 **teaspoon grated lemon peel**
1 **tablespoon lemon juice**
1 **cup sugar**
3 **eggs, well beaten**
1¾ **cups all-purpose flour**
¼ **teaspoon salt**
¾ **cup dried currants**

In a large mixing bowl, cream butter, lemon peel, and lemon juice until light. Add sugar; cream until light and fluffy. Add eggs; blend well. In another bowl, mix flour and salt; gradually add to creamed mixture, beating until well blended. Stir in currants. Drop batter by teaspoonfuls onto a greased and floured baking sheet. Bake at 350° F. for 10 minutes or until set. Remove from baking sheet to a wire rack to cool.

Bear Paw Cookies
Makes about 3 dozen

1 **cup butter** *or* **margarine, softened**
⅔ **cup sugar**
½ **cup chocolate-flavored syrup**
2 **eggs**
1 **teaspoon vanilla**
2⅓ **cups all-purpose flour**
2 **teaspoons baking powder**
1 **teaspoon salt**
¼ **cup milk**
Peanut halves *or* **cashews**

In a large mixing bowl, cream butter and sugar until light and fluffy. Blend in chocolate syrup. Add eggs, 1 at a time, beating well after each addition. Blend in vanilla. Combine flour, baking powder, and salt. Add dry ingredients alternately with milk to chocolate mixture, beating well after each addition. Cover and chill 1 hour. Drop batter by heaping teaspoonfuls onto a greased baking sheet. Press 4 peanut halves into each cookie. Bake at 375° F. for 10 to 12 minutes or until centers spring back when light touched. Cool on the baking sheet 2 minutes; transfer to a wire rack to cool completely.

Dark Chocolate Drop Cookies
Makes 4½ dozen

½ **cup butter** *or* **margarine, softened**
1 **cup packed brown sugar**
1 **egg**
1 **teaspoon vanilla**
2 **squares (1 ounce each) unsweetened baking chocolate, melted and cooled**
2 **cups all-purpose flour**
½ **teaspoon baking soda**
¼ **teaspoon salt**
¾ **cup dairy sour cream**
½ **cup chopped pecans**
Mocha Frosting

In a large mixing bowl, cream butter and brown sugar until smooth. Blend in egg, vanilla, and chocolate. Stir together flour, baking soda, and salt. Add dry ingredients alternately with sour cream to chocolate mixture, beating well after each addition. Stir in pecans. Drop batter by teaspoonfuls 2 inches apart onto a greased and floured baking sheet. Bake at 350° F. for 10 minutes or until set. Remove from baking sheet to a wire rack to cool. Frost with Mocha Frosting.

Mocha Frosting

¼ **cup butter, softened**
2 **tablespoons unsweetened cocoa**
2 **teaspoons instant coffee granules**
¼ **teaspoon salt**
3 **cups powdered sugar**
3 **tablespoons milk**
1½ **teaspooons vanilla**

In a medium mixing bowl, cream butter, cocoa, instant coffee, and salt until smooth. Gradually add powdered sugar, milk, and vanilla. Beat until frosting is smooth and of spreading consistency.

Drop Cookies

Vermont Drop Cookies

Makes 8 dozen

¾ **cup maple syrup**
¾ **cup packed dark brown sugar**
4 **eggs**
¾ **cup vegetable oil**
1 **teaspoon vanilla**
1 **cup skim milk powder**
2¾ **cups quick-cooking rolled oats**
1 **cup wheat germ**
1 **cup golden raisins**

In a large mixing bowl, combine maple syrup, brown sugar, eggs, oil, and vanilla; blend well. Stir in remaining ingredients in order given. Drop batter by teaspoonfuls onto a greased baking sheet. Bake at 350° F. for 12 to 15 minutes or until set. Remove from baking sheet to a wire rack to cool. Store in refrigerator.

Fruit Swirls

Makes about 3 dozen

¾ **cup vegetable shortening**
¾ **cup granulated sugar**
¾ **packed brown sugar**
1 **egg**
1 **teaspoon vanilla**
2 **cups flour**
1½ **teaspoons baking powder**
¾ **teaspoon salt**
½ **cup raspberry preserves**

In a large mixing bowl, cream shortening and sugars until smooth. Add egg and vanilla; blend well. Stir together flour, baking powder, and salt. Gradually add to creamed mixture; blend until smooth. Stir in raspberry preserves until just blended. Do not over-blend. Drop batter by teaspoonfuls about 2 inches apart onto an ungreased baking sheet. Bake at 375° F. for 12 to 15 minutes or until lightly browned. Remove from baking sheet to a wire rack to cool.

Chocolate Acorns

Makes 5 dozen

3 **egg whites**
1 **tablespoon vinegar**
¼ **teaspoon salt**
1 **cup sugar**
1 **teaspoon vanilla**
½ **pound ground blanched almonds**
4 **squares (1 ounce each) unsweetened baking chocolate, melted**
1 **cup semisweet chocolate chips, melted**
½ **cup finely chopped pistachio nuts**

In a large mixing bowl, beat egg whites until soft peaks form. Add vinegar and salt; continue beating. Gradually add sugar, beating until stiff peaks form. Fold in vanilla, almonds, and melted unsweetened chocolate. Drop batter by rounded teaspoonfuls 1 inch apart onto a greased baking sheet. Bake at 250° for 25 to 30 minutes or until set. Remove from baking sheet to a wire rack to cool. Dip half of each cookie into the melted chocolate chips; sprinkle with pistachios.

Shaped Cookies

Almond Slices
Makes about 7 dozen

1½ cups sliced unblanched
    almonds
2 cups all-purpose flour
1 cup sugar
1 teaspoon ground cinnamon
1 cup butter, softened
2 eggs

In a large mixing bowl, combine almonds, flour, sugar, and cinnamon. Add butter and eggs; blend well. Divide dough in half. Shape dough into 2 long blocks 3 inches wide. Wrap in plastic wrap and chill overnight. Cut dough into ⅛-inch slices. Place about 1 inch apart on a baking sheet. Bake at 375° F. for 10 minutes or until edges are lightly browned. Remove from baking sheet to a wire rack to cool.

Chocolate Pecan Tarts
Makes about 4 dozen

½ cup butter *or* margarine,
    softened
2 packages (3 ounces each)
    cream cheese, softened
½ cup vegetable shortening
2 cups all-purpose flour
    Chocolate Pecan Filling

In a large mixing bowl, cream butter, cream cheese, and shortening until smooth. Gradually add flour; blend well. Cover and chill until firm. Shape dough into 1-inch balls. Place balls in ungreased miniature muffin cups. Press firmly onto bottom and up sides of muffin cups, set aside. Prepare Chocolate Pecan Filling. Spoon a heaping teaspoonful of filling into each tart shell. Bake at 350° F. for 20 to 25 minutes or until tarts are golden brown. Cool in pan on a wire rack.

Chocolate Pecan Filling

2 eggs
¾ cup sugar
3 tablespoons cornstarch
½ cup butter *or* margarine,
    melted
1 teaspoon vanilla
2 tablespoons light corn syrup
¾ cup miniature semisweet
    chocolate chips
½ cup finely chopped pecans

In a small bowl, combine eggs, sugar, and cornstarch; blend well. Blend in butter, vanilla, and corn syrup. Stir in chocolate chips and pecans.

Pecan Butter Balls
Makes about 3 dozen

1 cup butter, softened
½ cup powdered sugar
½ teaspoon vanilla
1¾ cups all-purpose flour
½ cup chopped pecans

In a large mixing bowl, cream butter and sugar until light and fluffy. Blend in vanilla. Gradually add flour; blend well. Stir in nuts. Cover and chill until firm. Shape dough into 1-inch balls. Place on a greased baking sheet. Bake at 350° F. for 20 minutes or until golden brown. Remove from baking sheet to a wire rack to cool.

Sugar Cookies
Makes 6 dozen

1 cup granulated sugar
1 cup powdered sugar
1 cup butter *or* margarine, softened
1 cup vegetable oil
2 eggs
1 teaspoon baking soda
1 teaspoon cream of tartar
½ teaspoon salt
1 teaspoon vanilla
4½ cups flour
  Granulated sugar

In a large mixing bowl, combine sugars, butter, oil, and eggs; beat until well blended. Beat in baking soda, cream of tartar, salt, and vanilla. Gradually add flour; beat until well blended. Cover and chill well. Roll dough into 1-inch balls. Roll balls in granulated sugar. Place balls 2 inches apart on a baking sheet. Flatten with the bottom of a glass. Bake at 375° F. 10 to 12 minutes. Cool on a wire rack.

Snow-Covered Gingersnaps
Makes about 3 dozen

¾ cup shortening
1 cup granulated sugar
4 tablespoons molasses
1 egg
2 cups unsifted all-purpose flour
2 teaspoons baking soda
1 teaspoon salt
1 teaspoon cloves
1 teaspoon cinnamon
1 teaspoon ginger
  Powdered sugar

In a large bowl, cream shortening and sugar. Add molasses and egg, beating well after each addition; set aside. In another bowl, sift together flour, baking soda, salt, and spices. Add to creamed mixture to form dough. Roll into balls the size of a walnut. Roll balls in powdered sugar. Place on ungreased cookie sheet. Bake in a preheated 350° F. oven for 10 to 12 minutes. Sprinkle with powdered sugar before removing from cookie sheet.

Walnut Crescents
Makes about 5 dozen

1 **cup butter, softened**	In a large mixing bowl, cream butter and sugar until smooth. Add vanilla; blend well. Gradually blend in flour; stir in nuts. Shape spoonfuls of dough into rolls about 3 inches long. Place on an ungreased baking sheet. Pull ends down to form a crescent. Bake at 350° F. for 15 to 16 minutes or until golden. Cool slightly on pan. Remove to wire rack to cool completely. Dip ends in Chocolate Glaze, then in jimmies or coconut.

1 **cup butter, softened**
¾ **cup sugar**
1½ **teaspoons vanilla**
2½ **cups all-purpose flour**
1 **cup finely chopped walnuts**
Chocolate Glaze
Chocolate jimmies *or* **flaked coconut**

In a large mixing bowl, cream butter and sugar until smooth. Add vanilla; blend well. Gradually blend in flour; stir in nuts. Shape spoonfuls of dough into rolls about 3 inches long. Place on an ungreased baking sheet. Pull ends down to form a crescent. Bake at 350° F. for 15 to 16 minutes or until golden. Cool slightly on pan. Remove to wire rack to cool completely. Dip ends in Chocolate Glaze, then in jimmies or coconut.

Chocolate Glaze

1½ **ounces semisweet baking chocolate**
1½ **teaspoons light corn syrup**
1½ **teaspoons cream**

In a small saucepan, combine all ingredients. Cook over low heat, stirring constantly until smooth.

Crisp Chocolate Rolls
Makes about 3 dozen

½ **cup butter, softened**
½ **cup sugar**
1 **teaspoon vanilla**
2 **egg whites**
⅔ **cup all-purpose flour**
Creamy Chocolate Filling

In a large mixing bowl, cream butter, sugar, and vanilla until light and fluffy. Add egg whites; blend well. Gradually add flour; blend well. Drop batter by teaspoonfuls 1 inch apart on an ungreased baking sheet. Spread with the back of a spoon into 3-inch rounds. Bake at 375° F. for 5 minutes or until edges are light brown. Working with 1 cookie at a time, loosen from baking sheet with a spatula and then quickly roll tightly around a pencil. Transfer to a wire rack to cool, seam side down. With a pastry bag, soda straw, or wooden pick, fill rolls with Creamy Chocolate Filling.

Creamy Chocolate Filling

3 **squares (1 ounce each) semisweet chocolate**
¼ **teaspoon vegetable oil, butter,** *or* **margarine**

In a small saucepan, melt chocolate and oil over low heat, stirring constantly.

Date-Nut Roll Cookies
Makes about 3 dozen

2 cups brown sugar
1 cup shortening
3 eggs, well beaten
4 cups enriched flour
½ teaspoon salt
½ teaspoon soda

In a large bowl, cream sugar, shortening, and eggs; set aside. In another bowl, sift together flour, salt, and soda. Blend into creamed mixture and mix well. Divide dough into 4 parts; roll each out to ¼-inch thickness, and spread filling over all. Roll up each part, wrap in wax paper, and chill in refrigerator several hours. Cut in ¼-inch slices and bake on an ungreased cookie sheet in a preheated 375° F. oven for 12 minutes.

Filling

2 packages (8 ounces) dates, chopped
1 cup sugar
1 cup water
1 cup chopped pecans
¼ cup chopped candied cherries
¼ cup chopped candied pineapple

In a saucepan, cook dates, sugar, and water over low heat for 10 minutes. Stir in nuts, cherries, and pineapple; let cool.

Pinwheels
Makes about 7 dozen

¾ cup vegetable shortening *or* butter/shortening mixture
1 cup sugar
2 eggs
1 teaspoon vanilla
2½ cups all-purpose flour
1 teaspoon baking powder
1 teaspoon salt
2 squares (1 ounce each) unsweetened baking chocolate, melted and cooled

In a large mixing bowl, cream shortening and sugar until smooth. Blend in eggs and vanilla. Stir together flour, baking powder, and salt. Gradually add dry ingredients to creamed mixture; blend well. Divide dough in half. Blend chocolate into one half. Cover and chill both doughs until firm. Roll each dough into a 12 x 9-inch rectangle. Place chocolate dough on top of plain dough. Roll to about ¼ inch thick. Roll up from the long side. Wrap in plastic wrap and chill until firm. Cut into ⅛-inch slices. Place on an ungreased baking sheet. Bake at 400° F. for 8 to 10 minutes or until set. Remove from baking sheet to a wire rack to cool.

Molasses Cookies
Makes about 6 dozen cookies

1 **pound brown sugar**
2 **cups molasses**
1 **cup shortening**
2 **teaspoons ginger**
2 **teaspoons cinnamon**
1 **teaspoon salt**
1 **teaspoon baking soda**
½ **teaspoon cloves**
½ **cup boiling water**
2 **pounds flour**

Mix brown sugar, molasses, and shortening together in large bowl. Add spices; blend well. Mix in boiling water. Gradually blend in flour, making a stiff dough. Roll out very thin, cut with cookie cutters, and place on greased cookie sheets. Bake in a preheated 350° F. oven 8 minutes. Cool and store.

Brown Sugar Icebox Cookies
Makes about 5 dozen

1 **cup packed dark brown sugar**
1 **cup granulated sugar**
3 **eggs**
1½ **cups vegetable shortening**
4½ **cups all-purpose flour**
2 **teaspoons baking soda**
¼ **teaspoon salt**
1 **teaspoon ground cinnamon**
1 **cup chopped pecans**

In a large mixing bowl, combine sugars, eggs, and shortening; cream until light and fluffy. Stir together flour, baking soda, salt, and cinnamon. Gradually add dry ingredients to creamed mixture; blend well. Stir in pecans. Divide doughs into thirds. Shape each third into 1½-inch wide log. Wrap in plastic wrap and chill overnight. Cut dough into ⅛-inch slices. Place on a greased and floured baking sheet. Bake at 375° F. for 8 minutes. Watch carefully: these cookies burn easily. Remove from baking sheet to a wire rack to cool.

Grandma's Peanut Butter Cookies
Makes about 5 dozen

1 **cup butter** *or* **margarine**
1 **cup peanut butter**
1 **cup granulated sugar**
1 **cup packed brown sugar**
2 **eggs, lightly beaten**
1 **teaspoon vanilla**
2 **cups flour**
1 **teaspoon salt**
1 **teaspoon baking soda**

In a mixing bowl, cream butter and peanut butter until well blended. Add sugars; cream until light and fluffy. Beat in eggs and vanilla. In a separate bowl, sift together flour, salt, and baking soda. Gradually add to creamed mixture; blend well. Roll dough into 1-inch balls. Place balls, 2 inches apart, on a large baking sheet. Press with tines of a fork to flatten. Bake at 350° F. about 10 minutes or until golden. Cool on a wire rack.

Pink Party Sandwiches
Makes about 4 dozen

1¼ **cups butter, softened**
2 **cups sugar**
2 **eggs**
1 **teaspoon vanilla**
1½ **cups sifted all-purpose flour**
1½ **cups cornstarch**
½ **teaspoon cream of tartar**
   Pink Butter Filling

In a large mixing bowl, cream butter and sugar until smooth. Blend in eggs and vanilla. Stir together flour, cornstarch, and cream of tartar. Gradually add flour mixture to creamed mixture; blend well. Chill dough until firm. Roll out dough on a lightly floured surface to ⅛-inch thickness. Cut out with a floured 3-inch cookie cutter. Place on a greased baking sheet. Bake at 400° F. for about 8 minutes or until edges are golden brown. Remove from baking sheet to a wire rack to cool. Fill cookies with Pink Butter Filling.

Pink Butter Filling

¼ **cup butter, softened**
2 **cups sifted powdered sugar**
¼ **cup whipping cream**
1 **teaspoon vanilla**
   Red food coloring

Cream butter until light and fluffy. Gradually beat in sugar, cream, and vanilla. Tint with red food coloring. Beat until filling is of spreading consistency.

Cherry Thumbprints
Makes about 3½ dozen

1½ **cups all-purpose flour**
¼ **cup sugar**
½ **cup butter, softened**
1 **egg**
1 **teaspoon vanilla**
¼ **teaspoon salt**
¼ **cup finely chopped nuts**
1 **teaspoon grated lemon peel**
   Powdered sugar
   Cherry Filling

In a large mixing bowl, combine flour, sugar, butter, egg, vanilla, and salt; blend well. Stir in nuts and lemon peel. Gently shape dough into 1-inch balls. Place on an ungreased baking sheet. Press thumb deeply into center of each ball. Bake at 350° F. for 10 minutes or until cookies are set. Remove from baking sheet to a wire rack to cool. Roll cookies in powdered sugar. Prepare Cherry Filling. Spoon one cherry into the center of each cookie. For best results, fill cookies on the day they are to be served.

Cherry Filling

1 **can (16 or 17 ounces) pitted dark sweet cherries, drained; reserve ⅓ cup juice**
2 **teaspoons cornstarch**
   Dash salt

In a saucepan, combine reserved cherry juice and cornstarch. Add salt. Cook over medium heat, stirring constantly until thickened and clear. Stir in the cherries. Let stand until cool.

Index

BARS

Almond Squares, 48
Butterscotch Frosting, 44
Chocolate Chip Butterscotch Bars, 44
Chocolate Glaze, 46
Cream Cheese Frosting, 40
Date Chocolate Chip Bars, 44
Double Chocolate Crumble Bars, 48
English Toffee Bars, 41
Filbert Chocolate Cream Bars, 41
Fruit Bars, 46
Irish Mist Bars, 45
Jeweled Coconut Chews, 46
Mint Frosting, 41
Orange Bars, 43
Peanut Brittle Bars, 43
Pear and Graham Cracker Bars, 43
Pumpkin Bars, 40
Raspberry Bars, 45
Spice Bars, 45

BROWNIES

Best Fudge Nut Brownies, 37
Blonde Brownies, 36
Chocolate Frosting, 36
Light Nut Brownies, 36
Marshmallow Pecan Brownies, 39
Mocha Chocolate Frosting, 39
Moist Chocolate Brownies, 39
Toffee Crunch Brownies, 37
Two-Toned Brownies, 37

CAKES

Almond Chiffon Cake, 29
Apple Streusel Cake, 28
Carrot Cake, 32
Carrot Cake with Pineapple, 33
Chocolate Dream Cake, 28
Cranberry Glaze, 29
Cream Cheese Frosting, 32
Double Boiler Frosting, 29
Frosty Icing, 31
Frosty Spice Cake, 31
Glazed Williamsburg Pound Cake, 29

Honey Cake, 34
Honey Nut Topping, 34
Lemon Glaze, 33
Old-Fashioned Pound Cake, 31
Plum Crazy Cake, 32
Potato Cake, 34
Yeast Pound Cake, 33

DROP COOKIES

Anise Drops, 52
Applesauce Cookies, 52
Bear Paw Cookies, 53
Chocolate Acorns, 54
Cranberry Charms, 51
Currant Cakes, 52
Dark Chocolate Drop Cookies, 53
Drop Sugar Cookies, 49
Fruit Swirls, 54
Golden Apple Cookies, 51
Mocha Frosting, 53
Thumbprint Cookies, 49
Vermont Drop Cookies, 54

PIES

Deep Dish Strawberry-Rhubarb Pie, 26
Fresh Cherry Pie, 26
Lattice, 22
Lemon Lattice Pie, 22
Pecan Pie, 24
Piecrust, 22
Pink Ribbon Apple Pie, 25
Plum Pie, 24
Rhubarb Custard Dessert, 25
Sour Cream Pumpkin Pie, 26
Sweet Potato Pie, 24

QUICK BREADS

Applesauce Nut Bread, 14
Apricot Bread, 14
Blueberry Coffee Cake, 12
Carrot Bread, 16
Cinnamon Coffee Round, 13
Dark Pineapple Date Bread, 13
Date Bread, 16
Lemon Bread, 14
Pumpkin Bread, 16
Quick Orange Coffee Cake, 12
Streusel Topping, 13

ROLLS AND MUFFINS

Banana Muffins, 19
Bran Muffins, 21
Breakfast Rolls, 20
Cinnamon Rounds, 20
Cranberry Orange Muffins, 21
Oatmeal Muffins, 21
Pecan Rolls, 19
Poppy Seed Muffins, 17
Savory Bread Rolls, 17

SHAPED COOKIES

Almond Slices, 56
Brown Sugar Icebox Cookies, 61
Cherry Filling, 63
Cherry Thumbprints, 63
Chocolate Glaze, 59
Chocolate Pecan Filling, 56
Chocolate Pecan Tarts, 56
Creamy Chocolate Filling, 59
Crisp Chocolate Rolls, 59
Date Filling, 60
Date-Nut Roll Cookies, 60
Grandma's Peanut Butter Cookies, 61
Molasses Cookies, 61
Pecan Butter Balls, 57
Pink Butter Filling, 63
Pink Party Sandwiches, 63
Pinwheels, 60
Snow-Covered Gingersnaps, 57
Sugar Cookies, 57
Walnut Crescents, 59

YEAST BREADS

Almond Bread, 11
Braided Fruit Bread, 6
Cheese Bread, 8
Dilly Bread, 9
Good Egg Bread, 9
Hearth Bread, 8
Herb Bread, 11
Oatmeal Bread, 4
Raisin Braid, 5
Sesame Twist, 6
Mini-Loaves, 5
Wheat Germ Bread, 11
White Bread, 4